MARCHING FROM FAILURE TO SUCCESS

MARCHING FROM FAILURE TO SUCCESS

ANKUR KULKARNI

GYAN

Published by

GYAN

Gyan Publishing House
5, Ansari Road
Daryaganj, New Delhi-110002
Phone: 011-47034999, 9811692060
E-mail: books@gyanbooks.com

Distribution Network
gyanbooks.com
India, USA, Canada, UK, Australia, France

ISBN: 978-93-7169-261-8 (HB)
First Published, 2025

Printed at: Gyan Press, Delhi.

MARCHING FROM FAILURE TO SUCCESS

Author: ANKUR KULKARNI

CONTENTS

CHAPTER - 1

PREAMBLE

Success and failure are considered to be highly subjective terms per se. If we delve deeper, we are able to objectively streamline the concepts into holistic realms thereby rendering the terms relatable and connectible.

It is also claimed, albeit with certain element of doubt, that the two phenomena, that is, success and failure are basically in the mind or the psyche as such and it is our mental framework that inherently decides the outcome of every effort or endeavor, we undertake. The legendary basketball player Michael Jordan was once suspended from his school team and he used this failure to reach high echelons and turned the small failure into a big success. Transformation of a small failure into a big success or the same small failure into a bigger failure purely and surely depends on the way a person perceives the situation, analyses it and comes out with a plan of action on the same thus deciding the modus operandi and the follow up on the same.

A leading Hollywood actress, many years ago, when she was probably going through a lean phase, or we can call it suffering from failure, in a bout of severe depression, hired a paid assassin and gave him a handsome sum of money and asked him to shoot her. The assassin, ironically a compassionate man, heard her patiently and calmly told her that he thinks she should rethink on her decision and wait for a week. He promised to come back on the same day in the following week and complete the assignment if she still felt the same about life. The actress agreed to wait for a week. The assassin came back on the promised date and lo and behold the actress had drastically changed her mind towards the positive. ☺ ☺

Failure by its very nature is a temporary phenomenon unless we allow it to take gigantic proportions and become huge leading to negative manifestations like irritation and depression leading it to become an obstacle and create huge problems.

From the age of 23 when he suffered his first failure to the age of 52 when he eventually became the president of the United States of America, Abraham Lincoln never allowed the innumerable failure to dampen his motivation even for a split of second.

The iconic Bollywood superstar, Amitabh Bachchan, at the peak of his stardom did not give any interviews to the media thus shunting them off and when he had a downslide when he started his business venture ABCL and suffered a huge financial setback, the same media had a field day criticizing his decisions and tearing apart his failure. This definitively points to the fact that we should treat people

well, when we are successful so that they will treat us well when we are undergoing a spell of failure. It is well-nigh impossible to imagine now that Amitabh was rejected by All India Radio on the pretext that he had a weak voice, the same voice we are now in awe of being baritone and commanding. Many resounding flops before his first big hit ZANJEER did not allow him to let these small failures get in the way of astounding success.

If you are reading this book then surely you must have encountered some obstacle or deemed failure on the way and must have found it tough to deal with, and that is where this book can also be deemed as a manual will be of immense value and support in the march towards success.

Working on our weakest points and trying to turn them into our probable strengths is one of the most logical ways to ensure success. The pioneer of the automobile industry, Henry Ford, started early as an entrepreneur in his life thus ensuring that he had a head-start in his pursuit for the desired success in his chosen domain. Hence, being proactive and starting early also improves the chances of success to a great extent. As the proverb goes "the early bird catches the worm" so if we estimate with precision and plan meticulously for the foreseen as well as unforeseen challenges, we shall be protected from many undesirable results.

The legendary leg spinner B. Chandrasekhar had polio in his right hand but he used the defect to his advantage and utilized the lurch in the arm to pick up a whopping 242 test wickets.

Innate and immense faith in the power of the almighty in the face of tremendous pressure opens many new avenues towards success. In spiritual terms we call it a "leap of faith" which may seem a bit impractical but is actually quite pragmatic in its outline.

At times we have a strong feeling or perception that in-spite of being highly skilled and talented we find ourselves unable to match up financially to people who might not be as skilled or talented as us and still they are doing much better monetarily. As a part of the vision of this book, we shall strongly endeavor to create a roadmap with specific steps so as to enable the reader to have a holistic and concrete plan ready to be able to match to those financially superior with an innate sense of satisfaction and fulfillment so as to be able to remove the grouse that one has not got his due. For those who are slightly spiritual in nature, financial richness may not be that vital a parameter yet one has to understand that financial enrichment does add to the stature and gives an inherent sense of confidence leading to betterment of the standard of living overall.

Once a disciple went to the enlightened Osho and said "I think you are the guru of the moneyed only." Osho benignly

smiled and said softly, "Indeed I am, because, the one who can`t even earn good amount of money should not be my disciple". We may or may not agree or give consent to his words but indeed it has a certain wisdom associated with it which shall give us an insight into the importance of the monetary vitality in the modern-day context of being successful even if we are not deeply covetous of it . ☺ ☺

The entrepreneur par excellence, Steve jobs, at one time did not even have the basic need of food being fulfilled and he had to walk as much as seven kilometers to get a decent meal at the "Hare Rama Hare Krishna Temple" in the US, yet it never let it demoralize him and he rose to great heights.

Even after being the founder of APPLE, he was removed from the company by certain high-ranking officials, yet it did not disorient him and he founded a new company called PIXER. Later on, he took over apple again and made sure that both the entities scaled the heights exponentially. This example amply proves that temporary setbacks should not

be taken in deep earnest rather the ultimate objective should take prominence and be of paramount importance.

This book, in sense, aims to impart sequentially and with specific steps wherever possible, a robust guideline for initiating the journey towards success.

Seven C for Success

This book will give you a few takeaways, through upcoming chapters. These chapters will be giving thrust on following SEVEN C, which will pave a road for you towards success, glory and self-respect. Whenever I see dull eyes, lack of confidence among youth, I feel that something must be done to help them to reach where they deserve.

If you will follow the Techniques, Methods and stepwise process elaborated in this book, then no one can stop you from attaining the enduring success. Read all the steps, instructions and rigorously follow it till the attainment of your goal. Your subconscious mind may provide you an action plan, in the beginning or after sometime during the reading of the book. It will flash in your mind like a thought while you are awake or during your sleep as a dream. Keep observing and follow these ideas or thoughts. For attaining the glorious success, you must focus on following SEVEN C;

1. Coaching
2. Character
3. Communication
4. Commitment
5. Contagious Energy
6. Caring
7. Consistency

❄❄❄❄

CHAPTER - 2

ACTION PLAN

It is quite imperative that one has a clearly chalked out action plan in the pursuit of success. The steps to be followed need to be lucid and limpid and one has to maintain the absolute sanctity of the procedure if one has to be reaching the desired state of success. For that one has to be ready to sacrifice something precious and valuable to be able to reach the objective. Let us take our respected Prime Minister Shri Narendra Bhai Modi for example.

Years back, when he embarked on his journey towards reaching the pinnacle, he clearly decided that he will sacrifice his personal pleasures in order to accomplish his goal of changing the face of the Indian Democracy per se. He even abandoned his wife to attain the desired state of success as per his visionary paradigm. He did not indulge in luxuries nor did he while away his time in collecting materialistic pleasures.

All because he was crystal clear in his psyche that he wanted to make his homeland a corruption free and prosperous country. An immaculate and sacrosanct value system shall be immensely beneficial for the continuous march towards success as it will definitely invite the divine blessings and benediction which shall empower the soul and strengthen the resolve and dissolve the insecurities leading to a positive output in the holistic sense.

In this endeavor of his, he clearly chalked out a consolidated set of ethical and moral values which immensely helped him tide over the obstacles he encountered while

on his way to reach the desired echelons. The objective was totally PIOUS and hence the supernatural powers also combined to help him accomplish his targets with plan.

He honed his oratory skills to such an extent that he was able to exemplify his thoughts amply and with judicious eloquence and achieve his aims through concerted efforts. People started believing in him, his words and his ideology with fervor and hence he was able to successfully carve his niche to such an extent that he rose from being a PRACHARAK to being the CHIEF MINISTER OF GUJARAT and ultimately became the PRIME MINISTER OF INDIA. He steadfastly decided not to sleep more than 4 – 5 hours per day so that he is able to utilize more and more time to his task and strive stringently towards the same and the results are there in front of us for all to see.

Similarly, the legendary actor, director RAJ KAPOOR had decided that till he was essaying the role of a lead actor in movies, he would only consume DAAL PAAV, BOILED

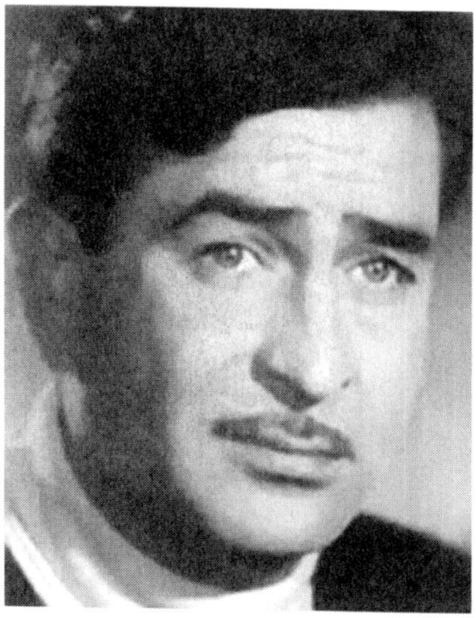

EGG for lunch- given his propensity to put on weight if he ate oily and fatty food- and hence, he was to play the lead for close to three decades. This amply proves that to acquire something valuable, one has to sacrifice something equally precious.

Thus, decisive decision making would be immensely beneficial in this pursuit. For this a clear and unprejudiced mindset is needed because any kind of bias which sets in will make us partial, in a sense rendering the deciding mind to be lopsided and the decision thus taken to be oddly balanced rather than being justifiably even. The repercussions and implications should be intricately studied and viably and feasibly imbibed and discerned in detail so as to avoid committing errors and blunders in the pursuit of success.

Another pertinent example in this context would be the iconic cricketer Mahendra Singh Dhoni, who in his school days was almost equally good at both football as a

goalkeeper and cricket as a wicketkeeper, but he consciously chose cricket over football as his career and vocation, since he realized that it would be cricket rather than football which will provide him the opportunity to scale the zenith of fame and popularity as well as provide him the financial security needed as an Indian sportsperson.

He steadfastly stuck to his goal of making his wicket-keeping and batting skills so vital for every team he represented that ultimately, he became an invaluable asset at times for his keeping and at others for his batting.

Prioritization is another key to success which holds tremendous significance in the overall scenario. At times, we get confused as to what to choose and hence end up losing many golden opportunities which would otherwise lead us to strategic benefit and profit. Say for example if we have to choose between growth or money, we end up dilly dallying at times becoming neither higher in profile or richer in financial terms.

Rather than thinking in terms of good or bad or right or wrong if we focus on what is apt {PROPER + SUFFICIENT} we will invariably find ourselves taking better and more appropriate decisions as per the goal intended. In the Mahabharata, Arjun had the choice either to choose Lord Shrikrishna or to go for The Narayani Sena. He very aptly and swiftly chose Lord Shrikrishna because he was fully aware that the side which had the blessings of the Lord could not possibly lose and the results are well known to all of us.

One must, first of all, do an objectively logical self-analysis or SWOT ANALYSIS so as to put it in the perspective. The accurate and pinpoint conditioning of one's STRENGTHS, WEAKNESSES, OPPORTUNITIES, THREATS will lend a lot of strength in the endeavor towards realizing the caliber and potential needed to achieve the success as per the person's ambitions, aspirations, desires, dreams.

People like Bill Gates, Steve Jobs, Michael Dell had chalked out a mental strategy whereby they had decided early that by the age of twenty or twenty-five they will have an entrepreneurial venture ready to roll and thereby they were able to formulate a clear plan and thereafter implemented and executed the same and accomplished their targets satisfactorily. They had a clear idea of where they were starting from and where they had to reach. Hence all their energies and enthusiasm were fully focused on that centrifugal point making it a comparatively smooth passage towards the goal.

A clear-cut plan day wise, week wise, month wise and finally year wise should be comprehensively prepared with apt illustrations and intricacies. Thereafter, one has to religiously adhere to the schedule and flow with the set targets and periodically evaluate and rectify any anomalies and lacuna which may be encountered during the practicing part. One should prepare a mission and vision statement cohesively and chart out a limpid action plan which shall be the guiding light for the march towards success.

It should list out in details like the exact target + the means to achieve it + the expected deadline by which it shall be achieved and the supporting people and accessories that shall be required in reaching the same. A clear and objective assessment and realization of one's major strengths and how they can be best utilized to gain momentum will give a huge fillip to the task in hand. Let us take for example that we realize that we are immensely good at grasping and absorbing concepts and understanding the nature of people than we may use these skills rather strengths to proper use and ripen them to such an extent that they become the catalysts and harbingers in the creation of the path towards success. Identify, hone, implement, analyze, carve your niche and keep improving on the same.

Thereafter, an honest appraisal of our areas of improvement, or weaknesses as we call them normally, will be hugely beneficial for the holistic development of the individualistic skills and temperament leading to the evolution and transformation of the vision and mission in a manner that shall exponentially enhance the chances of the accomplishment of the desired objective.

The strength of the value system enriches and enhances the overall fabric and structure of the entire endeavor towards success and enlightens the path in a manner that a permanent imprint can be created vibrantly glowing the sense of achievement and accomplishment.

The famed industrialist N. R. Narayan Murthy {one of the seven founders of the iconic software organization INFOSYS} was employed with PATNI COMPUTER SERVICES when he decided to be an entrepreneur and hence put down his papers as an employee with PATNI while he was working with on a crucial project. He could have left the project midway but his strong sense of ethics and robust value system did not allow him to do so. What he did was that he worked on that project for SEVENTEEN MONTHS WITHOUT SALARY and saw to it that it was completed in the right earnest☺ ☺. Another pertinent example of Murthy's value system is that when INFOSYS was being founded there was a heated debate as to what should be the core value system of the organization?? Someone said "WE SHOULD BE THE HIGHEST PROFIT MAKING COMPANY "while yet another founder suggested that "WE SHOULD BE THE ORGANIZATION WITH THE

MAXIMUM PROJECTS." Murthy simply smiled and said "WE WILL BE THE MOST ETHICAL AND PROFESSIONAL ORGANIZATION AND YOU WILL SEE THAT ALL OTHER FACTORS SHALL ALIGN THEMSELVES WITH THIS VALUE". PROPHETIC WORDS INDEED ☺ ☺ ..

In the master plan preparation of the objective, one should be quite careful in what one thinks, believes and perceives. As is widely quoted "BE CAREFUL OF YOUR THOUGHTS FOR THEY WILL BECOME YOUR ACTIONS; BE CAREFUL OF YOUR ACTIONS FOR THEY WILL BECOME YOUR HABITS; AND; BE VERY CAREFUL ABOUT YOUR HABITS FOR THEY WILL END UP BECOMING YOUR DESTINY". Therefore, we must give adequate thought to whether the thought to be thought is worth the thought ☺ ☺ .

The philosophy of Karma, as intrinsically enunciated in the Shrimad Bhagwat Gita, is the crux, essence, gist of our every action and its result and repercussion. The action must be well prepared, aptly noble, genuinely sincere and viably productive and only then will we be able to grasp fully the manner and the mode through which we shall reach our intended goals.

"FIRST, WE MAKE OUR HABITS AND THEN THE HABITS EITHER MAKE OR BREAK US". Ironically stoic yet the gospel truth. The habits we formulate as we grow up more or less define our persona, fortune, destiny. For example, if the habit to respect our elders and give them due recognition and adhere to our sacraments has been inculcated at an early age in us, then we shall always find that this will hold us in good stead as we tread on the path of our lives. On the other side, if someone has imbibed the values of domination and manipulation early in their lives, it will be well-nigh impossible for them to change their modus operandi at a later stage try as they might because the basic fabric has been intricately corrupted in a way that it has got ingrained deep into the psyche. Honesty, sincerity, punctuality, diligence are a few virtues which, if turned into habits, give a rich aroma of confidence, and decisiveness in the pursuit of every target we yearn for.

The action plan should imperatively list in a clear chronology the following:

1. The daily objectives
2. The weekly targets
3. The monthly goals
4. The annual objectives

As objectively as possible, we should assess our successes and failures on these parameters.

We MUST have to write down our sermon of life, i.e. an ultimate Goal which we want to achieve on paper or in a diary. The Goal must be well defined along with the stepwise action plan. We have to split major Goal into small parts of minor Landmarks along with time frame. That sermon we must read (if possible, loudly) every day in the morning and before going to bed.

This repeated activity will help our subconscious mind to believe that we will be achieving our goal soon and subconscious mind will continue to act upon it, till it becomes reality. While writing sermon we have to ensure that the objective is not vague- it must be very clear and along with the time line.

❄❄❄❄

CHAPTER - 3

FAITH

The essence of our life and success is basically dependent on our faith. As a toddler and then a child we have almost complete faith in our parents. We have complete and innate trust in the almighty as well. As a kid we believe with great innocence and purity in the goodness of things per se and totality of the same was vividly etched and accepted with all the intricacies understood and accepted. All our aspirations and desires were resultant of the apparatus so designed that it inherently propelled us to generate the strong-willed filled faith in the probable accomplishment of the targeted aims, targets, goals and objectives. As we grew up, we started to get more and more skeptical about the trustworthiness of things in their eventuality and existence which led to the shaking of the concept at times which is highly detrimental in the march from success to failure.

Selfish motives overpower the inherent value system of faith to such an extent that the very existence of the theory gets into jeopardy leading to complications. Let us remember in right earnest the historical example of Bhakt Prahlad if we have to deeply inculcate faith in our veins. His father, the mighty king *Hiranya-kashyapu* was arrogant to the point that he started considering himself to be a greater power than Lord Vishnu and told all his near and dear ones to start worshipping him and not Lord Vishnu.

Bhakt Prahlad, who had unflinching faith in the divinity of Lord Vishnu, steadfastly refused to accept and obey this dictate of his mighty father.

Enraged at this refusal, *Hiranya-kashyapu* employed various devious means to end the life of Bhakt Prahlad like mixing poison in his food and making him sit in fire but the firm faith did not allow the child to suffer any damage.

It has been noticed that even miracles are possible if one does not forego the faith. During the 1983 cricket world cup in England, nobody gave the Indian Cricket Team any chance of going beyond the group stage but due to the insurmountable faith of the young 24-year-old captain in the capability and the potential of his team, we not only reached the semifinal and the final but ACTUALLY ENDED UP WINNING THE WORLD CUP. ☺ ☺

Mahatma Gandhi's prime weapon in his struggle for the independence of India from the British rule was his immense faith in the purity and surety of his goal. He never lost the faith that ultimately the objective will be accomplished, come what may and hence all his energies

and willpower was fully concentrated on this target leading him to objectively attain level after level of the ambition.

Another beautiful example is the faith of PROPHET MOHAMMED who, despite being illiterate, was able to give the concept of university because he had immense faith in the goodness and power of education. The strength he derived from the faith ensured that he was able to guide and motivate his followers to steadfastly adhere to the value system thus inculcated in the psyche.

Faith is essentially the antidote to the apprehensions, doubts, suspicions which may otherwise crop up in the mind while pursuing any activity which requires consistent and tedious efforts. It builds an impregnable shield around which we can formulate and execute the fortified module of success which shall be quite beneficial and valuable for the eventual hoorah ☺ ☺.

Faith is not about change; it is essentially about transformation. Change can be positive or negative whereas transformation is always positive and hence faith would qualify in the category of transformation and not change. The child trusts her or his teacher implicitly and explicitly because the faith is clearly there that the transformation will be visible in the persona and the future will be distinctly bright.

We should periodically sit at a quiet place at peace with self and analyze who are the people we can implicitly trust and have faith in so that they can be our support systems for the journey towards success. Let us take for example that someone decides to start the march towards being a successful political leader he / she should be ready to sacrifice some essential luxuries and comforts and be ready to work on an average 14 – 16 hours a day and build a huge contingent of followers and supporters.

One should inculcate, develop and enhance immense and unassailable faith in one's own caliber and potential with a clear directive to brain repeatedly that "I WILL DO IT", with precision and objectivity so that the message gets repeated with sincerity and cements the structure. The conscious repetition of the thought shall deepen the resolve unflinchingly and deepen the conviction. The lacuna and shortfalls between the current and the desired state should be clearly identified and streamlined in such a manner that a fastidious roadmap can he decisively created and highlighted with the perspective and paradigm outlined specifically.

Temporary failures do not affect us much if faith as an ingredient is ingrained with appropriate depth. It will help us tide over the difficulties and obstacles with elan as it will be like a shield protecting us from the unforeseen hurdles which may crop up at unprecedented places. The development of the faith shall take place by giving repeated instructions to the mind at regular intervals and reiterating the salient features with the intricacies and nuances specifically charted out. Faith is an antidote, which when added enables us to have direct communication with the supreme power i.e. Almighty God.

Chhatrapati Shivaji Maharaj regularly reminded himself that his endeavor to establish SWARAJ is over and above all. Moreover, he told his followers and Sardars categorically that he is only a medium in the overall target not the source and hence they should use their acumen and pool all the resources to build up the forces and channelize the strength.

Faith begets divine blessings and intervention when faced with dire circumstances and hence that extra slice of intervention and motivation can be derived almost magically to strive on towards the desired destination with tremendous gusto and vigor. It gives us the verve that we shall eventually overcome the situation because our faith connects us with the forces above in a manner which amplifies the thrust. It gives us the assurance that whatever be the current circumstance we shall be able to overcome it and come out all smiles ☺ ☺.

Faith removes the cobwebs and illusions in the mind and generates absolute clarity so as to help us be lucid and limpid about the path to be followed that enable us to reach the desired state and destination. It makes us aware of the reality with its implications and charges.

While reading this book, keep following the instructions, keep repeating them and revising the basics in details. Make sure to keep at it regularly so that a concrete consolidation of the theory and practice can be established. The necessary and the essential and the vital and the compulsory and the mandatory can be distinctively differentiated and worked upon once we have developed the faith in a nutshell. If we only give the instruction once, the mind will not feel the intensity of the activity or the task in hand and the zeal with which the efforts are being done. Faith will bring the things in order and the tasks can be pursued in the right earnest and the results will be taken to the next level via the diligent and energetic efforts.

❄❄❄❄

CHAPTER - 4

4M -THE FOUR ESSENTIALS OF SUCCESS

While turning our life from upside down, bring transformation within ourselves and for that one must understand the vital foundations that will take us to the glorious future. The stronger the foundation, the longer will success last. In this topic we will discuss about Four Essential foundation stones of success. If we miss any of these four essentials, then we may achieve success but it will not be long-lasting or it will be vulnerable to failure.

The four essentials, 4M, while marching from failure to success are as follows:

1. MIND {MENTAL FITNESS}
2. MONEY {MONETARY FITNESS}
3. PHYSICAL FITNESS MUSCLE AND
4. MANPOWER i.e. TEAMWORK

MENTAL FITNESS

First of all, let us discuss the supreme power in the human body that is the mind. We can call it mental fitness as well. It is the one entity which completely monitors and maneuvers the other organs and senses with complete suzerainty. All the positivity as well as the negativity emanates from the mind itself and leads all the subsequent actions and niceties. It is the most active and volatile tool which effectively makes or mars the proceedings in totality.

Once a man was lying down idle beneath a tree at noon and just staring at the clear sky. A Friend of his was passing by and he saw the man lying. He stopped in his tracks and approached his friend and asked "Why are you lying here?? Get up and do some work". The lying man calmly replied "what will happen then ??". His friend said "You will earn money." Again, the lying man asked "What will happen then ??". The friend replied "You will have a family". Again, the lying man asked "What will happen then??". The friend replied "You will be able to relax". The lying man replied with contentment "THAT IS EXACTLY WHAT I AM DOING NOW ☺ ☺ ". IT IS THE MIND WHICH IS THE HARBINGER OF ALL THAT TRANSPIRES WITHIN AND OUTSIDE.

Mental fitness ensures that the concentration and focus levels reach the optimum and maximum levels and genres thereby allowing us to generate the desired levels of efficacy, efficiency and productivity.

One fundamental rule for building mental strength is with an exercise routine. Write down our objectives and goals and check whether we can stick with them. You may find these instructions very elementary and fundamental ideas. But researchers have proved that diet and regular physical exercise has very deep impact on our life and responses to the situations. It provides precise and valuable insights into our attitude and behavior. Healthy diet and regular physical exercise are the two foundational modalities over which we can develop and build mental strength and resilience.

Yoga and meditation go a long way in enhancing and enriching the mental faculties in such a manner that the onus of aims and targets and goals and objectives gets subtly gelled in a nuanced manner with the caliber and potential thereby desired. Whenever we are in distress, the mental stability is the discerning factor between those who give up and those who are able to come out of the disturbing situation with élan. A very famous poet once said that even when he was at the lowest rung of his career and almost wiped out, he never gave a thought to leaving because his mind constantly, day after day, month after month, gave him the fillip to hang on and keep going on. The mind formulates, evaluates, generates, recreates and keeps us either on our toes or brings us to our knees ☺ ☺.

The mind directly connects with the supernatural forces and enthuses the soul enriching the whole gamut of the emotions and recharging the acumen. It is the brain that guides us, enlightens us, builds up the strength and informs us as to how we should deal and encounter different situations and occurrences. Faith, trust, hope, belief all are offshoots of the mind only and hence we should all be in the absolute positive mindset hence enabling the objectivity to be optimized and the negativity to be erased.

There are many techniques available for meditation. Seating calmly, quietly and by just observing the moment of breath enables us to calm down our mind and attain Tranquility.

Monetary fitness

Money or monetary fitness is the next topic for discussion on our agenda. Starting on a lighter note, someone has quoted intrinsically "money is probably not everything, possibly, it is the only thing" ☺ ☺. While we may not entirely agree with the aforementioned thought, we also cannot ignore or neglect the relevance and depth of it, especially in the modern context and scenario.

Savings, systematic investment planning, cutting corners, being frugal are all under the umbrella of monetary fitness. Maintaining a steady flow of income and the wise distribution of the same is paramount to being robust financially and not having to worry permanently about how to meet the expenses. Whenever purchasing something, we should minutely scrutinize whether the purchase is actually necessary with regards to its longevity of use or in other words its durability in comparison to the cost or the price we are paying.

We should objectively and logically divide the incoming amount into separate heads and adhere to them religiously.

For Example – Say one fifth of our income can be directly sent to the savings account preparing for a rainy day, so as to say. Another one fifth can be spent judiciously for the betterment of our family so that the happiness quotient can be retained as consistently high ☺ ☺. The next one fifth can go for the benefit of the society or those who are in need and approach us for help thus fulfilling our accountability as a responsible human. The fourth one fifth can be straight away allocated to the daily needs like ration, food, milk and so on because these are quite essential for the existence as such. And then, the final one fifth can be well utilized for investing into future related occupancies be it shares / debentures / mutual funds so that a decade or two down the line we may not have to face monetary turmoil with respect to having ignored investments.

The proper allocation of funds as per the income generated will always yield excellent productivity and a broad long-term base for being financially secure. Money is basically the seed which if sown properly can grow into a very lucrative tree giving fruit and shelter throughout us life and be an essential ingredient in our march from failure to success ☺ ☺.

Muscle power

We always hear that strong mind and strong body are complementary. If we are mentally strong, our health will be good. Similarly, if we have good health, then naturally we will have good stress bearing capacity.

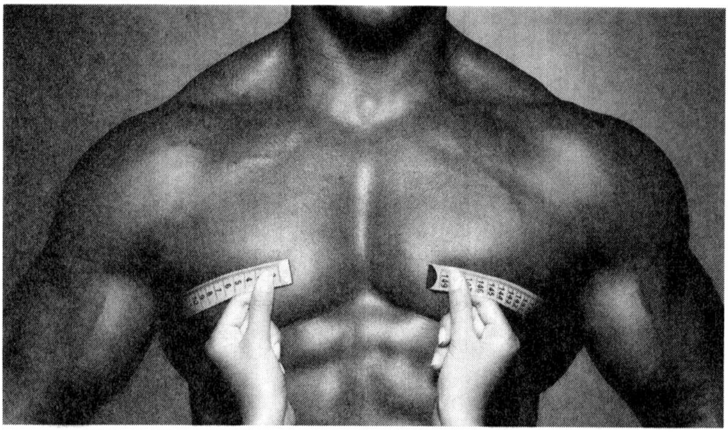

And then comes the muscle power, or strengths, as we may term it otherwise. In our march towards success, the skills we build up + the experience we acquire + the exposure we gain + the authority we accumulate all go a long way in ensuring that our sturdiness immaculate and we exponentially evolve and keep transforming into better selves.

Yoga enables resilience of the body, but in-order to maintain physical fitness and ability to perform the task within stressful circumstances we must earn strong body. These muscles will help us to overcome difficult situations and will enable us to work for prolonged years while attaining and enjoying the success. Physical fitness will boost our confidence and enhance our overall performance.

Manpower Or Teamwork

Nobody can achieve noteworthy success alone. He has to form a Master Mind Group or Team. The **TEAM** itself is having its full form as **T**ogether **E**veryone **A**chieves **M**ore. While selecting the team members we have to identify their attributes which will be complementary in achieving our goals.

Manpower or supportive associates and colleagues will always be powerhouse of energy for us as we strive for success in our lives. Our first support system is always our parents who selflessly groom and guide us from the day we are born till they are practically able to do so and even beyond. Our commitment towards respecting them, obeying them and imbibing the sacraments being inculcated by the parents should be absolute and complete.

Next come our teachers in school who are the storehouse of manners, etiquettes, values and morals which stand us in good stead basically throughout our lives. We shall all agree, probably, that our basic DNA in terms of thinking and executing was formulated during our school times only and thereafter it is mostly garnishing and brushing up of these ethics which we are doing for the remainder of our lives.

Further, our professors in college / university drill the value of quality and knowledge which forms the platform for our career on the horizon and how to deal with the various complications and complexities which shall probably be encountered by us during our careers.

As we initiate our march into our respective careers, we are surrounded by a plethora of colleagues and superiors, some of whom become ardent admirers and staunch supporters helping us rise and also tide over the obstacles. On the other hand, there is very insightful quotation in profession which goes thus "people normally do not leave their jobs, they leave their bosses" ☺ ☺.

Hence it is quite vital to formulate and cement the professional associations and strengthen the bonds so as to ensure that they become vital cogs in our march towards success. Trust, faith, mutual admiration is needed in huge doses for constructing, cementing, adhering, maintaining the professional bonds. If we enjoy the unstinted support of a few genuine professionals, we shall never lack reliable advice and valuable suggestions.

❄❄❄❄

CHAPTER - 5

WORKING ON SUBCONSCIOUS MIND

The power of the subconscious mind should be explored for marching towards success. The power of the subconscious mind can give you the strength to convert your failure into success. As far as concerned about the mind, we have two categories of mind- one is the Conscious and second one is Subconscious. In day-to-day life, we are making decisions. We are doing so many activities consciously as a part of our conscious mind activities but our subconscious mind is also attentive and active all the time.

Are we insisting ourselves to work upon our mind-graphs? It is because- when we are passing through failures, our mind gets filled with various negative emotions and it becomes a big hurdle when we want to uplift ourselves from the current status to a successful person. During this time span, it is necessary to train and guide our mind so that all the negative emotions, feelings, thoughts should be eradicated, converted and transformed into positive emotions, then only, it is possible to attain the taste of success. In earlier Chapters, we have said that repetitive instructions should be there to train our mind.

Many researchers have worked on conscious and subconscious mind very minutely. In the observation, they found that conscious mind works when we are awake or we are in action, or we can say that when we want to implement the ideas. But the subconscious mind works day and night relentlessly, even when we are sleeping. Our success is based on what we conceive in our sub-conscious mind. It should be in our plan for getting success by providing continuous instruction to our subconscious mind. It's like the repetitive affirmations that where we have to go and what we want to achieve. Once our subconscious mind is convinced, it will start working on it.

Subconscious mind has limitless powers. The conscious minds have doubts, confusions and it have analytical ability but subconscious mind works on faith. We have to consciously develop the faith in our life. We have to prepare a basic action plan for giving instructions to our subconscious mind. When we get up early in the morning and when we go to bed, during both the occasions we have to pass instructions through actions. We must prioritize mental repetition of our plan, added with positive affirmations.

We have to do it repeatedly, continuously for days, weeks and months. Gradually mind will start working in the same direction as our affirmative instructions. It will initiate the spark of the thoughts and ideas in our conscious mind which will lead us towards our goal. This will make the process easy and planning would be clearer and focused.

Conscious mind works upon the physical things but subconscious mind can have the accessibility beyond boundaries and having enormous powers. For example, if you are able to control your subconscious mind you can communicate, with the person sitting very far from you, without any physical requirements. So, the crux is that the continuous affirmations of repetitive nature will lead us towards our success and developing the faith in our subconscious mind will perform wonders for us.

Whenever we want to understand the existence and working of subconscious mind, normally we illustrate it with one of the very common examples- learning to drive a Car. During the initial phase when we are learning to drive a car, we have to continuously focus on the Steering, Gear and Clutch etc. of the car. We are also worried about every minor hurdle, turning or obstacle on the road.

Once we have obtained mastery over the driving we don't need neither to focus on the process nor the minor obstacles on the road. Because in the later phase our subconscious mind takes the charge and we drive the car as a routine activity without making any conscious effort for driving. Our subconscious mind directs the body to change the gears, turn the body, while our conscious mind listens music or chats with fellow passengers.

Remember one thing that the subconscious mind cannot distinguish between real and imaginary. If you introspect daily activities, you will realize that 95% of our daily activities is performed by subconscious mind. Our subconscious mind continues to store each and everything that has ever happened to us, much like a gigantic computer.

The subconscious mind is reactive. It responds to the nature of your thoughts. When your conscious mind is full of fear, worry, and anxiety, these negative emotions created in your conscious mind start releasing signals to subconscious mind. When this happens, you can speak affirmatively and communicate your subconscious mind with a deep sense of authority to stop the irrational emotions generated in your deeper mind.

You will be fascinated to see what happens when you speak authoritatively, and with conviction to the irrational movement of your deeper self. Your mind will be flooded with Faith, Harmony and Peace.

In the 2009 hindi movie, Three Idiots, the concept of "All Is Well" is elaborated, which narrates that, one has to convince their subconscious mind that everything is fine. This gives psychological relaxation and gives energy and courage to face the real life problems.

The above example highlights the working of subconscious mind. Subconscious mind works on Faith. We need to understand, how to develop faith in our subconscious mind. Scientists have proved that there is only one way to influence the subconscious mind i.e. repeated instructions with complete faith. Remember our subconscious mind never sleeps, never rests. You can discover the miracle working power of your subconscious by plainly stating to your subconscious prior to sleep that you want a specific thing accomplished. You will be amazed and delighted to discover that the hidden forces within us will be activate in that direction, that lead us to the accomplishment of our desired Goal.

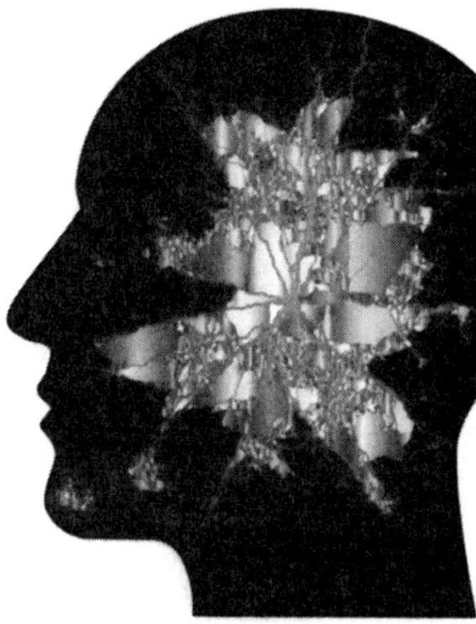

The activities performed by us will be understood and percolated by the subconscious mind with different experiences. Our subconscious mind works day and night. Whatever perception of subconscious mind about our personality and abilities- our dreams start functioning in our subconscious mind. For attaining success, we need to convince our subconscious mind then only we can attend the success.

The repetitive instructions will help to train our mind. Without it, it is difficult to achieve success. Without convincing the subconscious mind, we cannot deliver our best for accomplishing our decisions. We would not be feeling confident about success without the active support from subconscious level. If you convince your subconscious mind, the success ratio will increase drastically and you will definitely achieve whatever you desire. For attaining success, it is necessary to convince our subconscious mind. I am sure that you need to give again and again instructions to your subconscious mind for convincing it. Visualizing is very important to instruct our subconscious mind so when early in the morning or at night while you are about to sleep, you need to visualize those things which you want to attain in your life. Thus, gradually your subconscious mind will start thinking in that direction and you can find the answers to your difficulties and problems. You can find different alternatives for your difficulties and you can get the solutions to your problems as in these circumstances the subconscious mind will help you in various aspects.

Let's take the example of Mr. Narendra Modi, our Honorable Prime Minister. He must have given the instructions to his subconscious mind that one day he will be a top leader of India. Deliberate instructions are the requirements of your subconscious mind to program your mind for attaining success. When we start connecting with our subconscious mind, automatically we get the solutions to any problems of the world. Whatever we want to attain, the planning for the same will start taking shape in reality and with the help of our subconscious mind.

Miracles will start happening with us, too-when once we understand the power of subconscious mind and begin using the magic power of our subconscious mind. Our subconscious mind is having unlimited capacity. It is having ability of clairvoyance and clairaudience: It can visualize and listen to the events that are taking place elsewhere. It is having reach beyond the physical world.

Thus have a faith in yourself, in supernatural power God and start using the power within you to bring complete transformation in your current life. Be the change. You yourself can bring complete transformation in your materialistic and spiritual life.

❄❄❄❄

CHAPTER - 6

ETHICAL VALUES

"As you will sow, so shall you reap" goes the proverb. It is exactly how life goes. The ethical and moral seeds which are sowed since childhood are the catalysts for the genesis and evolution of our existence. If the ethical values are well ingrained and quintessentially robust than any stressful or traumatic situation can be handled calmly. Self-realization, acceptance of a mistake, a feeling of regret and guilt on a wrongdoing are all symbolic of a strong value system.

Amitabh Bachchan was in deep financial stress after the failure of his venture ABCL and had a long list of creditors. Dhirubhai Ambani came to know of his predicament and asked his younger son Anil {a close friend of Amitabh Bachchan} to help him out by offering a significant amount.

When Anil approached Amitabh with the offer, he expressed his deepest gratitude but politely declined the offer citing self-respect. Later on, when Amitabh went to Dhirubhai's birthday party, he called Amitabh to where he was seated with all industry giants, Dhirubhai Ambani pointed to all his friends *"Yeh ladka gir gaya tha, lekin apni lagan aur mehnat se phir uth gaya"*. It was the strong ethical value system that helped Amitabh Bachchan come out of his trauma.

For achieving any noteworthy and long-lasting success, fundamental ethical value system must be followed. People, the society and divine forces will definitely help us only if we are sticking to the fundamental ethical value system of Truth, Justice, Empathy, Honesty, Sincerity, Integrity, Loyalty. Because these things will set you apart from the crowd and you will be considered yourself as a brand.

ETHICS, VALUES, FAITH

Failure strongly tests our value system. If ethics and morals have been intrinsically inculcated in our sacraments, then it will be immensely possible to tide over the obstacles with ease and arrive at a fresh horizon with confidence. The character basically decides the vigor and exuberance with which we are able to deal with tough situations.

Loyalty to those around us and to the task in hand makes us appreciated and respected by those whom we rely upon and in times of need they are likely to stand by and for us. We should be careful not to create enemies because a hundred friends may or may not support us in trouble, but one deadly enemy would surely harm us as much as possible.

Integrity is another virtue which shall endear us and makes us trustworthy and liked. Saying what we mean and deeply meaning what we say is paramount to the establishment of our credentials as people with integrity. Backbiting should be clearly avoided so as to ensure our credibility.

Doing anything and everything to the best of our ability without thinking about the size and the magnitude of the task can be broadly summed up as sincerity. As they say very aptly, talent without sincerity is basically useless. If we imbibe sincerity as an integral part of our value system, we can establish our reputation impeccably and design a well-knit and strong structure so as to be able to work our way through the trials and tribulations in our march from failure to success.

Eagerness, earnestness, enthusiasm are virtues which help us a lot in life when we march from failure to success. As they say, lack of cosmetics may wrinkle our skin, but lack of enthusiasm wrinkles our soul ☺. Right from the initiation to the culmination, if we can successfully maintain and sustain our eagerness, we shall see a marked change in the result we are striving for.

Probably one of the toughest tasks in the world is to self-analyze objectively without any bias and prejudice. Periodically if we can practice self-analysis, realize our mistakes and errors and blunders and accept them in totality and start working on them in the right earnest it would be a great help in marching towards success. Self-introspection is an immaculate tool in this endeavor which shall enhance and illuminate the path whenever darkness surrounds us ☺ ☺.

Born in Greenfield Township, Michigan, in 1863, Henry Ford was the industrialist who started Ford Motor Company, which has been one of the most profitable automotive companies in the world over the years, making him one of the richest and most famous individuals on the planet.

However, while Ford celebrated many successes later on in life, he also failed often in his earlier years. In fact, it wasn't until 1891, when Ford was 28-years old, that he decided to become an engineer, working for the Edison Illuminating Company and earning a promotion in 1893 at the age of 30, to Chief Engineer. It was around this time when he started experimenting with gasoline engines. Ford established an automobile Company a year later in 1899.

In 1901, however, that company failed after an inability to pay back a loan to the Dodge brothers and due to inefficiencies in the design of the vehicle; the company ceased operations, dealing a stealthy blow to Ford. However, subsequently, Ford convinced one of these partners to give him another chance. With mounting pressure, it was agreed that he would try again. But after disagreements, this venture also flopped.

It wasn't until 1903, when Ford would give it one final shot. At the age of 40-years old, after two separate failures, he tried again, incorporating the Ford Motor Company. Even after the failures, Ford found an unconventional backer who he made agree not to meddle in the business. He found this in Malcolmson, a Scottish immigrant who had made his fortune in the coal industry.

Afterwards, what transpired is one of the most famous stories of an individual who went from failure to success in the grandest way. The Ford name is synonymous with the automobile. In fact, while the assembly line existed prior to Ford's arrival on the scene, so to speak, he created a car that was affordable by the everyday family, helping to develop what was to become the largest boon in the automotive industry with cars everywhere.

During the second world war when the United States of America needed war machines in bulk, the ford group offered all their premises for manufacturing of war planes and jeeps keeping aside any commercial gains. Thus, the strong value system ensured that THE FORD BRAND GAINED CULT STATUS ☺ ☺ .

It's true, despite his many failures, Elon Musk is not only a genius but also an incredibly motivated individual with a burning desire to succeed.

Tesla and Space X look certain to enjoy a successful future. It's testament to his character that we simply cannot doubt or image what the South African will do next!

When Elon first started out, he unsuccessfully applied to a number of emerging tech companies including Netscape. In light of these rejections, he founded a searchable business directory called Zip2 which was essentially an online version of a telephone book.

Believe it or not, PayPal was voted the worst business idea of the year in 1999. When it was released as a security software for the Palm Pilot and other handheld devices. However, Musk and co-founder Max Levchin started to focus on creating an online wallet which started to gain traction.

Many experts in the auto industry were very vocal about their disdain for Tesla when it first arrived on the scene. According to these individuals, the electric car was a non-starter certain to fail.

In 2008, it looked likely that these predictions would come true as Tesla stood on the brink of collapse due to insufficient finances. Musk was in the midst of producing the Model S at the time. Incredibly, he decided to go bankrupt and used his personal wealth to keep the company going.

His strong work ethic and value system made him what he is today and helped him tide over the difficulties with elan.

Born in 1890 in Indiana, Colonel Harland Sanders, the founder of Kentucky Fried Chicken (KFC), is famous not only for his chicken recipe, but also his numerous failures in life and in business. At the ripe young age of 5- years old, his father died, leaving only his mother to fend for and support three children, including Harland.

While his mother left for days on end, Harland was forced to help take care of his siblings and became a proficient cook during this time, learning how to make bread and vegetables and advancing in his knowledge of cooking and preparing meat by the age of just 7-years old.

By 10-years old, he was already working as a farmhand. In 1902, at the age of 12-years old, his mother remarried, subjecting the children to an arduous environment that ultimately forced Harland to leave home the following year.

By 14-years old, he began working as a farmhand at another farm in Southern Indiana.

Sanders worked odd jobs for years, never really able to make anything stick. He owned a ferry boat company on the Ohio River, sold tires in Winchester Kentucky, and later, in 1930, opened a restaurant inside a Shell Oil Company-owned gas station in North Corbin Kentucky where he began serving chicken dishes. He was 40-years old at the time.

In July 1939, he came to own a motel and a restaurant, which was destroyed by a fire just 4 months later. But it wasn't until 1940 when he began to finalize his so-called "secret" chicken recipe, at the age of 50. However, in 1942, during the war, he sold his business and subsequently got divorced in 1947.

In 1955, another one of his restaurants failed after an Interstate route that led traffic past that restaurant, was changed. That year, with just a $105 social security check to his name, at the age of 65-years old, he set out to sell his franchised-chicken model to restaurants across the country. He was famously rejected by 1,009 restaurants before one agreed to his idea.

❄❄❄❄

CHAPTER - 7

STRENGTHENING OURSELVES

The insurmountable inner strength is a sure shot stepping stone towards the quest for success. If the spirit becomes indomitable and the zeal becomes robust then no task is beyond us.

Nick Vujicic {Australian Evangelist} was born without fully formed limbs. According to his autobiography, his mother refused to see him or hold him when the nurse held

him in front of her. She and her husband went out of the hospital and vomited from seeing their son with no limbs, but they eventually accepted the condition and understood it as "God's plan" for their son.

Originally, the toes of one of his feet were fused. An operation was performed to separate the toes so that he could use them as fingers to grab. He refers to it as his chicken drumstick.

When he was seventeen years old, Vujicic's mother showed him a newspaper article about a woman praying with a severe disability; he then started to give talks at his prayer group.

Vujicic graduated from Griffith University at the age of 21 with a Bachelor of Commerce degree, with a double major in accountancy and financial planning.

His immense belief in the power of his inner core strength made him overcome the tremendous hurdles thrown by life at him.

The talented mountain climber Arunima Sinha was pushed from a running train by robbers in 2011 while she was resisting them, causing in rods pushed into her right leg and multiple fractures of the spinal cord. Her aim was to climb each of the continents' highest peaks and hoist the national flag of India. She has already done seven peaks till 2014 i.e. as listed: Everest in Asia, Kilimanjaro in Africa, Elbrus in Europe, Kosciuszko in Australia, Aconcagua in She recollects "I resisted and they pushed me out of the train. I could not move. I remember seeing a train coming towards me. I tried getting up. By then, the train had run over my leg. I don't remember anything after that."

Immediately, as she fell on the railway track, another train on a parallel track crushed her leg below the knee. She was rushed to the hospital with serious leg and pelvic injuries and lost her leg after doctors amputated it to save her life.

She was offered compensation of ₹25,000 (US$330) by the Indian Sports Ministry. Following national outrage, the Minister of State for Youth Affairs and Sports Ajay Maken announced an additional Rs. ₹200,000 (US$2,700) compensation as medical relief, together with a recommendation for a job in the CISF. The Indian Railways also offered her a job.

On 18 April 2011, she was brought to the All-India Institute of Medical Sciences for further treatment, spending four months at the Institute. She was provided a prosthetic leg free of cost by a private Delhi-based Indian company.

While still being treated in the All-India Institute of Medical Sciences, she resolved to climb Mount Everest. She was inspired by cricketer Yuvraj Singh (who had successfully battled cancer) and other television shows, "to do something" with her life. She excelled in the basic mountaineering course from the Nehru Institute of Mountaineering, Uttarkashi, and was encouraged by her mother to climb Everest. She climbed Mount Everest with a prosthetic leg, which was arranged by raising funds with the help of a swami of Ramakrishna Mission, Vadodara.

Arunima Sinha is an exquisite example of the power of strengthening the inner self to a point that success comes from within.

She contacted Bachendri Pal, the first Indian woman to climb Mount Everest, in 2011. When she met Pal and Arunima told her story to her, Bachendri Pal said to Arunima "My child, you decided to climb Mount Everest in these situations with Prosthetic (Artificial) leg. You had climbed, achieved Mount Everest my child now just the date is remaining to the World to know".

And after that, Arunima joined a basic mountaineering course from Nehru Institute of Mountaineering and TATA Steel Adventure (TSAF) in Uttarkashi (India) and she was encouraged or motivated by her elder brother Omprakash to climb Mount Everest. Sinha climbed Island Peak (6150 meters) in 2012 as preparation for her ascent of Everest.

Sinha and Susan Mahout, a USAF instructor, who had together climbed Mount Chaser Sangria (6,622 meters or 21,726 feet) in 2012 under the guidance of Hendrick Pal, started their ascent of Mount Everest.

After a hard toil of 17 hours, Sinha reached the summit of Mount Everest at 10:55 am on the 21st of May, 2013, as part of the Tata Group-sponsored Eco Everest Expedition, becoming the first female amputee to scale Everest. She took 52 days to reach the summit. She wrote a small message thanking the Almighty on a wrapped cloth and pressed it in the snow. Recounting the incident, she said:

> "It was my tribute to Shankara Bhagawan, and Swami Vivekananda who has been an inspiration throughout my life."

There was an extremely learned and wise teacher once who never taught anybody. What actually used to take place was that he stayed in a small hut in the forest. Whenever someone used to visit him and knock the door, he shouted from inside "Kaun hai ??" and naturally the person told his name and then the door did not open. One fine day an eleven-year-old inquisitive boy came to the hut and knocked. Naturally, the same question came from inside

“Kaun hai??”. The boy innocuously replied “Yehi toh jaan ne aaya hoon ☺ ☺”. The door opened quietly. The inner strength of the boy and his conviction was the reason why the door opened and he was able to succeed.

Dashrath Manjhi, also known as Mountain Man, was a laborer in Gehlaur village, near Gaya in Bihar, India. When his wife died in 1959 due to injury caused by falling from a mountain, he decided to carve a path of 110 m long (360 ft), 9.1 m (30 ft) wide and 7.7 m (25 ft) deep through a ridge of hills using only a hammer and a chisel. After 22 years of work, Dashrath shortened travel between the Atri and Wazirganj blocks of Gaya town from 55 km to 15 km.

Dashrath Manjhi`s example proves that intense inner resolve overcomes the lack of resources and materialistic facilities if the inner strength is at the optimum level.

Arnold Schwarzenegger began lifting weights at the age of 15 and went on to win the Mr. Universe title at age

20, subsequently winning the Mr. Olympia contest seven times; he remains a prominent figure in bodybuilding, and has written many books and articles on it. The Arnold Sports Festival, considered the second-most important bodybuilding event after Mr. Olympia, is named after him.

His rise to fame and glory is another pertinent example of the strengthening of the inner self. We observe fast on various occasions so as to strengthen the inner self and prepare ourselves to face the adversities of life.

During the 1970's and 1980's the fast bowlers from the West Indies were quite a terror and were known for bowling bouncers and beamers to terrorize the batsmen of the era. When the Indian team toured the West Indies during the era there was only one Indian batsman who faced them without wearing a helmet – THE LITTLE MASTER SUNIL GAVASKAR ☺ ☺. When asked why he did not wear a helmet, he simply smiled and replied "The helmet only provides an outer, artificial protection whereas my confidence and skill which are my natural strengths will help me overcome the pace of the West Indians" ☺ ☺.

We should objectively and fastidiously identify the areas where we are quite strong and ensure that we constantly build up those areas on a daily, weekly, fortnightly and monthly basis with a rational and objective analysis on the same with the distinct features comprehensively dissected and robustly built up. A small chart can be prepared and regularly updated as follows:

1. MAJOR STRENGHTS {MAXIMUM 3}
2. CURRENT SCORE {OUT OF 10}
3. SCORE 3 MONTHS BACK {OUT OF 10}

4. PROJECTED SCORE AFTER 3 MONTHS {OUT OF 10}

The inner self decides the level of persistence for success and resistance towards disappointment in our striving towards the objective.

Joan of Arc nicknamed "The Maid of Orléans" came from an obscure village and rose to prominence when she was a teenager, and she did so as an uneducated peasant. The French and English kings had justified the ongoing war through competing interpretations of inheritance law, first concerning Edward III's claim to the French throne and then Henry VI. The conflict had been a legalistic feud between two related royal families, but Joan transformed it along nationalist lines and gave meaning to appeals such as that of squire Jean de Metz when he asked, "Must the king be driven from the kingdom; and are we to be English?" In the words of Stephen Richey, "She turned what had been a dry dynastic squabble that left the common people unmoved except for their own suffering into a passionately popular war of national liberation." Richey also expresses the breadth of her subsequent appeal:

The people who came after her in the five centuries since her death tried to make everything of her: demonic fanatic, spiritual mystic, naive and tragically ill-used tool of the powerful, creator and icon of modern popular nationalism, adored heroine, saint. She insisted, even when threatened with torture and faced with death by fire, that she was guided by voices from God. Voices or no voices, her achievements leave anyone who knows her story shaking his head in amazed wonder.

The young girl had strengthened her inner self so much that ultimately her martyrdom also did not dampen her spirits and enthusiasm and it made her immortal ..

Lord Parashurama is described in some versions of the Mahabharat as the angry Brahmin who, with his axe, killed a huge number of Kshatriya warriors because they were abusing their power. In some versions, he even kills his own mother because his father asks him to in order to test his obeisance towards his parents. After Parasurama obeys his father's order to kill his mother, his father grants him a boon. Parasurama asks for the reward that his mother be brought back to life, and she is restored to life. Parasurama remains filled with sorrow after the violence, repents and expiates his sin.

After his mother comes back to life, he tries to clean the blood-stained axe but he finds a drop of blood which he was unable to clean and tries cleaning the blood drop in different rivers. This is when he moves towards the south of India in search of any holy river where he could clean his axe. Finally, he reaches Tirthahalli village in Shimoga, Karnataka and tries to clean the axe and to his surprise, the axe gets cleaned in the Holy River of Tunga. With respect towards the holy river, he constructs a Shiva linga and performs pooja and the temple is named as Rameshwaram temple. The place where Lord Parashurama cleaned his axe is called Rama Kunda.

There is a conscious mind and there is a sub conscious mind and it is always the combination of the two that leads one to reach the desired objectives. The conscious mind has many tools to observe like eyes, ears, nose and so on but the sub conscious mind is completely and totally dependent on the conscious mind. So, the conscious mind has to consistently and regularly feed the sub conscious mind so as to be in sync and strengthen the self.

A weekly, fortnightly, monthly, six monthly and yearly analyses should be done with a calm and composed mind to assess what has been the change in the self during this duration.

Focus is a key to succeeding here and as we discussed earlier in the book, it is essentially MIND, MUSCLE, MONEY, HEALTH which are the ingredients which propel the march towards success.

Yoga and meditation are natural and majestic modes to strengthen the inner self. Yoga means joining together and hence the different aspects are connected intrinsically with its help and accentuates the worth. Yoga helps immensely in the simultaneous activation of the body and mind, both of which are equally vital for the robustness of the self.

The mind, by its very nature, is overactive and keeps wandering and hence has to be given directions regularly with modulation and guidance in a manner that the synchronization with the body optimizes and maximizes efficacy.

The tranquility of the mind and the psyche is the barometer of the body's health in a certain way.

"The mind is fickle, it will not obey you every time, when it disobeys you use your discretionary intellect to bring it back to equilibrium position" – LORD KRISHNA. This quotation sublimely yet surely emphasizes the impact and importance of the need to be in complete control of the restlessness of the mind.

Bhagwat Subramanya Chandrasekhar was an Indian former cricketer who played as a leg spinner. Considered among the top echelon of leg spinners, Chandrasekhar, along with Prasanna, Bishen Singh Bedi and Srinivasa-Raghavan Venkata-Raghavan constituted the Indian spin quartet.

This Quartet dominated spin bowling during the 1960s and 1970s. At a very young age, polio left his right arm withered. Chandrasekhar played 58 Test matches, capturing 242 wickets at an average of 29.74 in a career that spanned sixteen years. He is the only test cricketers in history with more wickets than total runs scored, the other being Chris Martin.

He was awarded the Padmashri in 1972. The innate strength displayed by him during his life enabled him to tide over all the physical, emotional and other obstacles enroot to success.

❄❄❄❄

CHAPTER - 8

NETWORKING

The bonds we create, the closeness we generate, the associations we culminate are essentially the crux of the cementing of the relations we are able to stimulate.

In this era of the world fast becoming a global village, networking is quite essential for the channelizing of the resourcefulness into the desired direction thereby ensuring a permanent path towards success.

The best and easiest way to meet people is through referrals. Stick around with the people you already know and who know the people you are looking to meet. Being introduced through them or joining in with their conversations, you will very likely receive a warm welcome and introduction to the person you wanted an introduction to. This is a similar effect to LinkedIn through their online introduction tool, or even through joining the right circle at an event with somebody you know.

Before you start networking, be sure to have an agenda and keep the meeting on track. Time is money and people are never happy with someone that takes up too much of their time. By planning out your meeting ahead of time, you establish your professionalism, you gain credibility and cover all the critical topics you wanted to cover.

We gravitate and help those who are similar to us. Common ties extend beyond school. Coming from the same hometown, rooting for the same sports team, sharing unique backgrounds (like being a female engineer in marketing or having studied a non-traditional degree), even having the same name or birthday immediately warms people up to each other.

There are people who are supremely talented and skilled yet do not command the ability to connect and network well and hence, at times, are deprived of deserved success whereas there are others who are not that skilled or talented yet on the strength of strong networking skills are able to scale high echelons in their respective domains.

There are a couple of very famous brands named AMWAY and ORIFLAME who have earned huge portions of money purely on the strength of their ability to network with a large number of people and keep building the networks in such a manner that everyone connected benefits from the association making the bond robust and strong.

Every person we come in contact with has some unique feature with which we can connect, explore and gain from.

The happy, generous, valorous, close-knit associations we generate expunge most of the negativity that encompasses us whenever we are unable to deal with stressful and strenuous situations and instances. Be it our childhood or adulthood the networking is an essentially vital ingredient on the pathway towards success and we should constantly keep renewing and rebuilding the same.

Take for example the marketing and sales professionals. They will undoubtedly vouch for the fact that it is how effectively and efficiently they are able to build their network with existing and prospective customers that is the catalyst and the harbinger for their success in their domain. Even if there is little or no need for a product, at times, due to the strong network, the customer obliges with an order purely on the strength of the bond created.

In the classic cult hit SHOLAY when the character essayed by late Sanjeev Kumar titled THAKUR BALDEV SINGH want to search the characters called JAI and VEERU {played by AMITABH BACCHAN and DHARMENDRA} he simply called a much junior jailor who came all the way first by train and thereafter riding a horse because he had immense respect for the bond THAKUR WHO WAS EARLIER A SENIOR JAILOR had created with the much younger colleague.

From our scriptures and ancient history, we can quote innumerable examples of networking leading to immense benefits. The army which the epitome of morality LORD SHRIRAM led to Lanka was a supreme result of the networking prowess of LORD HANUMAN and SUGREEV who assembled a unique mix of VANARS, REECHH and ably guide by the wise JATAYU.

❄❄❄❄

CHAPTER - 9

OVERCOMING THE OBSTACLES

Whenever in life we try for major objective or major goal the national we are likely to come across. Every journey worth taking involves resistance. The higher the goal, the steeper the climb. Obstacles are not exceptions, they are the rule. But for those who overcome the them, these challenges become the very stepping stones to greatness. We are praying for such a big goal or Mission that we have to conduct our business opportunity straight and do SWOT analysis because this makes us ready to know our short pulse, then only we can. Maybe I would elect any other things it has to offer, so we all do as we are decided in the past.

Angela Duckworth, in her book *Grit highlights how perseverance and passion over time matter more than raw talent. It is not the most gifted who succeed, but the most who determined.*

Obstacles come in many forms: financial hardships, societal barriers, physical limitations, emotional trauma or even self-doubt often we confuse these challenges as signals to stop. But history and psychology suggest otherwise.

At 21, Stephen Hawking was diagnosed with ALS, a neurodegenerative disease, and given just a few years to live. The illness robbed him of almost all physical mobility. But it couldn't touch his mind.

We are having the weakness of the naturally, we should have enough strength. Anyone will reach at the top or anyone who will achieve their success, we should be in a position to acquire some sacrifices when will it be windy at 11 or you live at any rights after that if the literature of the video three sensors were at work but he is a very important one if we will repair the window there are few pieces which are predominant dominating to every form in person and a very important here is fear of death show me the important thing is that we have to accept that death is a reality an animal or living thing on this Earth so we have to accept that to the end of the day.

Obstacles are often perceived negatively as frustrating barriers often halt progress. Yet they can be reframed as opportunities, that guide us towards self-awareness and innovation. The difference lies in mindset. Some people take it. When confronted with obstacles some people crumble while others pivot and find alternative route to success. So, we need to correct ourselves and change our mindset.

Consider Oprah Winfrey, now a global media Mughal and philanthropist. Her early life was riddled with: poverty, abuse, and discrimination. As a young girl Oprah Winfrey was shuffled between relatives and faced significant hardships. But she didn't allow her past to define her future. Instead, she harnessed her experience, using them as fuel to become a voice for empowerment and positivity. Oprah once said "turn your wounds into wisdom." Her journey exemplifies how recognizing and accepting obstacles can transform pain into power.

One of the most paralyzing obstacles is fear of failure. Many avoid taking risks or pursuing dreams because they dread falling short. Though failure is not the opposite of success, it is part of journey towards it.

There are various things which we can do that, I want that one is very important financial planning amount with you. Make yourself which will make you self a convertible or relaxed in this Moment wisely, maybe in a real estate, maybe enlist in the goodies or so that you will not help, you will have a psychological confidence of overcoming the fear of poverty in the same time. You will have to accept that money is not everything and money is the most minor thing whenever you are at the window anymore. I'm trying to call you a couple of goals or visions or you may come across some potential losses for this will be temporarily because if you will have the inner abilities of your mental strength, your physical strength then you can overcome and you will find the history is full of such persons who have raised from the Ashes to the top Like a Phoenix, so that confidence you have to do love within yourself. If you want very big success in life, you will have to take the chances, when you are taking the chances, you may have come across looking at least your losses this doesn't mean that you should stop. Fight with your own abilities, which you will be delivering best on your support and assist those abilities will enable you to overcome those small repeats more losses to reach to the ultimate human or atonement of the goal of success.

Suppose you are having a minor defeat, if you are having a positive attitude then definitely you are going to win. You will try to learn from that and you will turn yourself off so that you will be in a position to attend more Glory without bring your mindset negative because you cannot overcome with a negative mindset. How to train your mind to think positively whether you are in a success or whenever you are at the pain. You have to see a list of positive side of that, because every failure will give you an opportunity to retrospect yourself, you grow better and more- brighter and aspire for more- bigger things. When we want to let you make things than that early it brings itself suppose it is a natural human tendency to how to peel anxiety or stress Whenever there is no change and that is why we have to accept as it is, because if there is a change in the atmosphere we will find stress, if there is a change in place we will find strength in the new people that will be stress so that stress is obvious and that will accept it as obvious thing then our mindset changes because stress is a part and parcel of our day- to-day life. It will be accompanying to stay but without stay there will not be anything or if you are alone and there will be stressed.

Very important thing is that you try to be proactive that way things are going to happen. If you try to anticipate, these things will happen, supposed to say you aren't willing to let the office, then I tell you how to accept that you are a superior or if you're upset with you and definitely day will be great if you want to. If you want anything, let you have that trouble just to bring some take you along with you this release will change the topic of the anticipation of that's just fully deliver a speech if you are going to enter into negotiations if you will be prepared. Louder pro-activeness, then naturally your stress level will be less, because you will be knowing that you are prepare thoroughly for the coming situation. To manage the stress, you have to do one more thing, doing yoga and meditation which will be acting as a reinforcement in your personality and your day could be like that will enable you to overcome and withstand the stress which you will be pissing in day-to-day life. Things which will be releasing your stress for timing but which will make you to Habitat for that such as jingle bell jingle all the way you will have to learn to manage the stress within yourself. By using the yoga and meditation, yoga postures regularly with a regular pattern in the morning or in the evening or during meditation in the morning or in the evening will enable you to strengthen your mind, and will be helpful to you, definitely to manage your stress and anxiety.

There is another important thing which we carry on with our past failures about the past mistakes and because of that we always carry that burden with us, something which we should not do. To release the burden from mind, meet the person if he/she is available to you and make that ecology to forgive the person and yourself too. When it is not possible then it is better that you should go to the church or go to the temple and talk with the almighty God and tell the things whatever you're committed and empty your mind so that you will be stress-free for performing the best.

❄❄❄❄

CHAPTER - 10

MANAGING FINANCE FOR SUCCESS

It's been years to listen that "Money is the Power". Thus, financial stability gives us peace and strength therefore we can overcome our obstacles and move forward towards success. We can say financial planning is crucial. If we have sufficient balance in our bank account, we feel confident and secured and our capability of taking risk also increases.

Either you may be changing jobs, taking a risk in business or any kind of business negotiations. So, we believe that for managing the finance, we need to plan in such a way that the amount available in our account, gives us enough strength to take the risk and boost up our confidence. When we plan our finance, we need to keep two points in our mind. The first one, recurring amount which is necessary for our day-to-day activities and other general expenses and the other one is for uncertain situations such as accidental conditions which can happen anytime for example- medical expenses or any accidental situation. As a reader of this book, you are striving for success. So, it is a principal to understand the value of money. Because if we will see the history, we observe that many persons although they were having various abilities due to lack of money, they will have to succumb to the persons who is stronger in their financial status. So, we need to underline that money is very important in our life and powerful as well.

According to some people, money is not much important. Yes, it is true that we can buy bed but not sleep but there are various things that money can enable in our life. For becoming a successful person, we need to be money conscious. That consciousness we need to bring in our daily lifestyle so that we can manage our decisions which we are taking towards success. If we are talking about an individual, we can measure the success based upon his or her financial status. Because money makes us avail so many things like multiple facilities, infrastructure and resources. In the beginning of this book, we have discussed three major powers – Money, Muscle and Mind. With this statement we can say that if you have the money power you can purchase the muscle power.

And for the peace of our mind, we need to have a certain amount of money which will give us the strength and satisfaction and definitely peace of mind. In your life you may have experienced the same thing that so many people have observed, that irrespectively having the caliber, intelligence and potential, due to lack of money the person is unable to excel in their lives just because of the money factor. So here, we can assure that money is also a kind of weapon, which we can use for our success. Yes, money cannot buy everything but it can buy something which can definitely give you the benefit in life.

Strategic planning of investment- We have to make strategic decisions because when we need money as a tool for

many types of expenses as per the plan so that we can take chances and we get some temporary values or temporary setbacks, in that case monetary strength will be there to give support during that time, so to plan it accordingly. For strategic planning of our financial management as rightly

said by Warren Buffett that "we should not keep all the eggs in the same basket" likewise we need to understand the concept and invest in different domains. It will give you success in the short terms and long-term goals both.

A wiser and smarter way should be adapted for investing and planning for our money and investment as well. Let's take an example of investment like you have 100 rupees for investing – 30% you should invest in fixed deposit in banks which is a sure and fixed kind of investment. Some money you can invest in equities which will give you higher returns but risk factor is also associated with it. So, it is advisable to invest around 25% in risk markets. We need to keep a few savings around 25% for any kind of emergency like medical expenses so we can access it any time within 24 hours.

We can invest 15% in Gold or SIPs also. As per my opinion, we should keep 5% percent of investment in charity as well. In that way it will come to us by different means, the returns would be higher. Everybody has experienced that charity brings prosperity. That is also a kind of investment which you are doing for yourself. Because it will give you best wishes and blessings which cannot be measured in monetary terms.

Short term-long term financial management–

Let's talk about short-term and long-term planning of finance of yours. Here we define that short term investment means 5 to 10 years planning of your expenses cum savings and long-term planning means 10 years / 20 years / 30 years of planning. As we have already discussed in the previous topics, short-term investment are like savings or FDs. Long term investment means investing in real estate or shares and equities. These long terms kind of benefits which are provided by the financial instrument in the market will give you assured returns without any risk but the duration must be long enough. Here we can take the example of insurance policies and long-term investment plans offered by the banks.

Pearls of financial wisdom

1. Bonds are for storing wealth and equities are for creation of wealth.
2. In my opinion, the biggest asset one can have is zero debt.
3. The greatest discipline in personal finance is living below your means.
4. As Ben Carlson says, emotions cannot be back tested. That's why past bear market always looks like opportunities and future ones scary.
5. Early financial independence and early retirement are completely different. To me, the former is a blessing and the latter is a curse.
6. Don't think how it would have been if you've started 10 years ago. Start today and visualize how you would feel 10 years from now.
7. The neighborhood we live determines our life style & spending. Need to be careful in choosing one which matches our goals and personality.
8. Paying minimum balance regularly on credit card is the maximum sign that you're getting into debt trap.
9. Many are long term investors till the next bear market.

10. Don't take aggressive bets. Take measured risk. Remember one blunder can push you back by a decade or more in terms of wealth.
11. Big money can be made through high savings, wise investing and lots of patience.
12. One sign of progress in an individual investor's portfolio is no churn or very less churn.
13. Trying to get rich fast is a foolproof way to lose what we have.
14. Losing opportunities is far better than losing money. Don't invest in fads.
15. "Making as much money as quickly as possible" is not an investment strategy. Unfortunately, for most of us, it is a strategy.
16. Aggressive strategy cannot be a substitute for high savings. Save high and take moderate risk then saving less and taking high risk.
17. The day we realize not losing is as important as winning; we would stop blindly chasing returns.
18. Good periods are more than bad periods. By not timing, though we go through bad periods, do not miss even a single good period.
19. We'll stop looking for quick money the moment we consider stocks as businesses and realize that our wealth grows in line with business growth.
20. There are periods of high returns, low returns, no returns and negative returns. We need to go through all these to get long term returns.

21. Listening to market forecasts is not only useless but can be very harmful too; if you start acting on them.
22. The hard truth is only around 3% of our population are in a position to aspire for financial independence. Don't waste this rare privilege.

There are lot of similarities in blood circulation and circulation of money. We are healthy only when blood is circulating freely in our body, similarly we are economically healthy, when money is circulating freely in our life.

Due to insecurity or stress when we begin to hoard money, to put it away in tin boxes, and become charged with fear, there is an economic illness. So, to be successful, keep investing and allow money to circulate wisely.

❄❄❄❄

CHAPTER - 11

DIGESTING THE SUCCESS

To attain success is easy but to digest it, is much more difficult than achieving it. The instance one starts getting the success, whether it is financial or in career path or in the profession, but certain times, people fail to digest the success. When we are preparing ourselves for achieving the success, we also need to learn how to digest the success because it is more important to digest than to achieve it. If the success comes with the obsession, it will definitely give you defeat or the day you start getting it with an obsession, you will face failure again and again. People used to get the success in a very short period of time but we have so many examples which show that it becomes difficult to carry the success along with them for longer period of time. For maintaining success, I previously talked about the strong ethical values which you can follow and then only you can sustain with success. Thus, it will not get converted into obsession. If we have basic ethical values like honesty, sincerity, discipline, hard work, genuineness, justice and transparency all these ethical values will give you strength and abilities to digest the success. ☺ ☺ ...

Many people get success by luck or fluke but for them it is difficult to handle, hold or carrying it. If the success is achieved through hard work and rigorous efforts, then the success is long lasting. If the success is based on the ethical values and personal ethics the success will be everlasting.

We have many live examples of people who got the success and it was just a momentous and they were not capable to carry and handle it for so long. The fear of failure always creates the feeling of insecurity. This feeling leads towards the wrong actions and for holding it more, people start involving in unethical practices. Those unethical activities again drag them towards their failures.

Let us talk about it with an example of a very successful celebrity and super star of an era Mr. Rajesh Khanna (The first super-star of Bollywood). He had achieved very noteworthy success and enjoyed the stardom and success

for quite a long time, till the day Bollywood got some professional works for him. The lack of professionalism, interpersonal skills, taking undue advantage of success and very poor time management gradually destroyed the career graph of the super star. If the person is able to realize in the early stage that he or she is losing the success and will take the corrective measures, then it is possible to sustain and hold the success for much longer period of time. But at that time, if you ignore the chances of facing, the downfall will increase.

Few successful persons used to realize it after failure then also it is not very late. It is just the matter of proper plan and corrective action to achieve those pinnacles. It might be difficult but possible. We must trust ourselves and move on. I would like to quote again the example of Mr. Amitabh Bachchan. It would be apt if we learn from his journey.

When Amitabh Bachchan was successful, he used to avoid media. Due to poor interpersonal relationships, when he tasted the failure, he realized the flaws and gradually

improved upon it. He developed a very strong professional attitude. Then he became media friendly and achieved excellent interpersonal skills. He had developed empathy towards others which has result him into a rise in his career in later ages.

If you are following unethical practices or adopting shortcuts you will land in trouble and face the difficulties one or the other day. So, it is important to follow the ethical practices without shortcuts, for everlasting success.

As we can refer many examples of politicians, they were at the top or at the glory but ended up with imprisonment due to unethical practices.

If our success is based on the ethical practices, basic principles, truth, justice, empathy, social responsibility, respect, rationality, and other traits related to the same, then it builds a strong and sustainable foundation. One more thing, I would like to mention its adaptability. If you are rigid and do not want to change, then everyone starts overlooking your qualities for which you are known for.

Just take the examples of once established brands like Xerox, Nokia and Kodak. Once upon a time these brands were at the helm of the industry and were enjoying a very big share of the market. But due to the rigidness towards change and lack of adaptability along with the changing market these brands lost the client base and failed terribly in the market.

For enduring success, we have to be always alert, ever evolving and resilient. Learning new technologies, languages keep us acceptable at every corner. Many times, people quit from the topmost position as they fail to embrace change in the management. Maintaining humbleness, adaptability enable us to get adjusted with the new leaders, technology and working systems. We should be adaptive in our Personal life and Professional life as well. Resilience and flexibility make our success long lasting.

If with the success, our aspirations for learning new things diminishes, then that success will not last long. We must remember that success is incidental happening and will give joy for very short duration. But the journey towards success is very long and if we will learn to enjoy the journey or the process, then it will motivate us to keep going from one successful apex to another- Because our goal will not be destination but the process.

If a person achieves the noteworthy success, he will become a brand himself. Former President Dr. A.P.J Abdul Kalam, Amitabh Bachchan, Narendra Modi, JRD Tata and many such persons have become a brand in themselves. Because of their simplicity, humbleness, discipline, adaptability, resilience, keen interest for new technology, social responsibility and ability to work hard, these persons have become a real hero and a big inspiration for all of us. ☺ ☺ ☺ ...

❄❄❄❄